Come Thunder

Barbara Helfgott Hyett

LILY POETRY REVIEW BOOKS

for my Grandgirls: Stephanie, Emily and Kayla, and for Jed.

This is not my home. How did I get so far from water?
It must be over that way somewhere.

Elizabeth Bishop

FOREWORD

Barbara had been telling me for years that a storm was coming, and then it came. Through the writing of *Come Thunder,* I watched her fight with her poems, fight with 40-year-old lines, some of which she never wanted to write but wrote because she had to, wrote because "what you write about, chooses you."

I am one of Barbara's readers, her student, and one of her loves. I began working with Barbara when I was just seventeen and the only classic I had read was Dante along with every poet that called themselves "a beat poet". As with most of her students, we quickly became close friends, and as my mentor she played a large part in how I made my way as a poet and person in this world. Once I started really flourishing as a poet— leaving out the truth because it isn't poetry, revise-revise-revise, publishing my first collection, taking any challenge she gave me, for example, writing a crown of sonnets— she asked me to help her finish her manuscript. She believed in me, my voice, my eyes and ears, my soul.

To put this book together, she and I sat at her workshop table every week— my mentor showing me her own creative process so I could take part in her revisions. She would always be my mentor, my friend, but now I was also her reader which she told me I earned. And in turn, I got to watch as she worked a poem into tercets. I watched her agonize over where the line should break. I sat with her through the pain of *would've* vs. *could've,* because the whole poem depended on it.

Barbara's process of writing *Come Thunder* made me a better poet. After we would meet for an all-day session, I would go home to reread every could've and would've I had ever written, and rearrange them. I spent hours contemplating my choices of this, that, the, a. Which is best with the noun that follows in terms of consonance or assonance? Which makes the image the most cringing, the most hard-hitting? Then, I would take my pages back to her so we could work on my poems in an intimate back and forth.

Although *Come Thunder* had been a lifelong project, these poems are poems of urgency. Many poems in this collection are works she'd been holding onto for years. In her first chapter, "Atlantic City", Barbara focuses on her early years, accepting that it may take one's whole life to finish childhood. Her Atlantic City poems allowed her to be in charge of that childhood. Barbara was able to revisit who she had been through careful craft, while still making each poem a solid reflection of who she is, a transformation she earned through a close reconsideration of herself. At one point she said she had written a "failed sestina," but all it actually needed was her forty-years-later self.

The newer poems scattered through the following two chapters recognize how everything is tangible, even in the face of a storm. *Come Thunder* is where Barbara let her lines get tangled. The same phrases, images, and similes show up poem after poem because yes, there is so much to say and so much to keep saying. The repetition works. The same line means something different every time.

Her son, Eric E Hyett, poet and translator, said of Barbara's one poem interlude, "Monarch in a Jar" (which was published in The Maine Review) "She wanted to convey the power of transformation, and explore what we hang onto, and how we let go of anything." This is one of her earth-shaking themes in this defiant collection that changed me as a writer and a being.

Barbara saved my life in so many ways with the presence of poetry. She taught me that saving one's life is the process of a poet, and that everything you write is written to save your own life in some way. Every poem she has ever written took bravery. For each poem in *Come Thunder*, Barbara entered the storm, and at the same time, emerged from the storm.

Alexis Ivy
June 2022
Boston, MA

CONTENTS

I. Atlantic City

1   Light Keeper's Daughter

2   All Night The Waves

3   The Summer My Mother Said She Was
         Going To Drown Herself

5   I Never Said I Love You Best

6   Fear of the Dark

7   Money

9   Making Do

10   High-Wire

11   Dead-End Street

13   Chloe Price Dance Studio

15   Puppeteering

16   The Christmas Show

17   Report Card

18   One Sunday

19   Pick-Up Games

20   Rented

23   My Brother's Closet

24   Health Class

26   I Should've Had My Nose Done

27   Lifeguard

28   Before Sputnik

29   Wartime

33   The Darkroom Man

35   Queen of the Nobodies

36   Comic Books

38   Painted Horse on the Carousel 0

II. Transparency

41   Monarch in a Jar

III. Proof of the Spinning World

49   Cro-Magnon: Day One

50   Steeplechase

51   The Work of Shoes

52   Things in Their Disorder

53   B'reshith, Revised

55   Concerning Slugs

56   Poem at Split Rock Cove

58   Before the Meteors

61   East Boston Federal Courthouse

63   Hard to Tell

64   Moth in Three Voices

66   To Be Happy

67   Blood. Breath. Whisky.

68   The Trouble with Wealth

69   The Generals

70   Boston Marathon Bombing, 2013

71   Falling

72   Boston, Midwinter

73   The Cat, Beauty

74   Last Evening

76   Walking Without an Umbrella in New York City

77   Floods

78   The Cliffs

79   Girl on a Wheel

80   After Reading Da Vinci's Notebooks

81   The Cat, Truth

82   Light Takes the Tree

84   Dinner Conversations

85   Fortune Teller

86   Latitude 40 North

87   To Be a Sloth

88   Night Guided by a Brown Beetle

89   Girl, Port Au Prince

90   The River Dure

91   Proof of the Spinning World

93   *Acknowledgements*

I. ATLANTIC CITY

Light Keeper's Daughter

Blinded by salt, she went out
into it, hand to the window
with a rag: vinegar, pail heft,
tumult while her brother, warm
enough in the stairwell, played.
The catwalk held as she turned
the way the light turned in its nest.
Clockwork: the whole world
a semaphore of sound. Her heart
was a chapel in that dark, *a love
so big it scared her.* Her hair
iced by sea: wild and fire and full
of the spit of life. Brave she was
and leaned on herself out there.
Light sending out its own raw
warning—*Red! Red! White!*

All Night The Waves

1.
My name is *Bedtime.* Everything
is on my floor. All night the waves.

All night the shouting.
I am alone among everything

on the floor. My small bed. My M
& M's. I am alone or maybe

there's a bear, stuffed flatly, not
growling, but a kind of motorized

grind from behind his red felt
lips. My name is Sleepy. The bear

will not be quiet. My parents
forget me from the living room.

2.
My name is *Morning.* On my street,
all the doors are open. Sometimes

they're closed. Sometimes there
are no grown-ups all day. We have

no keys. Nothing of mine
breaks here. The doors are

solid firmament and all
the keyholes, stars. The keyholes

kneel to see themselves. The sea
breathes every hour. I keep a plaid umbrella

on my doorknob. Sometimes I borrow.
Sometimes I make a poem of my life.

-after Michael Mack

The Summer My Mother Said She Was Going To Drown Herself

In the living room stood the turtle bowl
with its little ramp to nowhere. I'd stop
to look at the pink plastic terrazzo—

wouldn't touch even a leg of one
of them. Both of their backs were
painted scary. Now, and then

I'd feed them, pinch in some
fairy flakes from the orange tin. Then
one day they were gone. My mother

had no story to explain this. *Pets*,
she'd said they were. But I knew
she hated them—must have

taken them to the toilet when
I was sleeping, must have
flushed my little turtles down.

I Never Said I Love You Best

I suffered beside them,
the two bears my mother
pushed to one side
of my pillow, because
they crowd the bed.
I was just wanting to
sleep between them,
I worried—who
to bring closest to my ear,
who to leave
by the headboard? I loved
Squeaky best, the oldest
and barely still brown. So
much more did I love him.
But Reddy, carnival prize
my brother won for me,
Reddy, who was neither
soft nor pretty, how I
pitied him and dared not
hurt his feelings. I tried
to stay awake, denying
my dreams their outcome,
and longed for Squeaky.
Still, I talked to Reddy.
I love you, I told him.
Now go to sleep.
Sometimes he would,
and sometimes he
wouldn't, since he
couldn't really trust me.

Fear of the Dark

Which should I choose
to suffer: the roaches
hiding in the wall
behind my bed, or
let my taffeta
bedspread stay where it
slid onto the floor?
Who to call for help?
What if I cry? No!
Lie still in the wet
sheets, and count the waves
outside the window,
though it's hard to know
when one wave stops, and
and how soon the next
comes in. I know Dark
wants to hurt me. I
must talk to my bear.
And if he insists,
I'll sing—*and for me*
some scarlet ribbons,
scarlet ribbons for
her hair—

Money

Franklin fives, tens and twenties.
I'd watch my father slap

his earnings down, my mother
calculating with pen on paper

at our kitchen table, my father
like a king counting out his

money. On and on like that.
What did it mean, I'd wonder

after, in bed with the dark,
the lights of the fancy hotels

bearing down? Why go to work
so handsome, wear a felt fedora

and brown-belted gabardine coat?
To carry a beat leather sample

case—thin packs of cigarettes
and cigars to sell to hotel owners.

To share a cup of coffee in the
leatherette booth, then bring that

money home. To marry a bonus.
Mornings, frozen orange juice,

poached eggs on toast already on
the breakfast table. Where did all

that money go? I had my own
bonus piggy bank from Boardwalk

National Bank and Trust. I saved
nothing because that pig had no slot.

Making Do

Not everything is
possible but you
are a child and do
not know that, so you
set out to make a
paper airplane, but
have no balsa wood,
so you substitute
the bottom of the
box your ice skates came
in, and find you have
no rubber bands, just
a blue hair ribbon
to hold every thing
in place, and because
you have no paints, you
have to crayon the
airplane engine in,
but you don't really
draw very well so
it looks like a sad
refrigerator
instead, and you pour
some India ink
on until the cardboard
itself turns hard. But
how will you get
the ink off the top
of your own desk now?
I'll have to forget
this paper airplane
project. I'll never
be good, my Mother
tells me, *with my hands.*

High-Wire

O, the dying are such acrobats.
—Deborah Digges

When my mother joined the circus,
she played slide-piano under the Big Top,
learned tumbling from the Spanish family,

could roll and roll as if forever.
Lunchtime we'd marvel
at the Fire Eaters, and Tattoo Man

would muscle the crescent moon for me,
Then she'd practice swinging
on the trapeze. Sometimes

I'd dance beneath her on the sawdust,
or have to climb up partway, talk her
down. She was not quite fit for balance.

I could see that. Once I heard
the Bare Back Rider say,
the Fat Lady ought to stay on the ground.

Nights, in our car on the circus train,
I'd wash her feet for her, rub them dry.
I wasn't happy. I wasn't really sad;

relieved, I guess, or shy to be that close
to my mother. In our bed, I'd wall
my pillow between us—listen

to the horses sway like spun gold!
I had to learn to fend the lions off,
had to learn to love them.

Dead-End Street

We were weaned from grace early on. Sent
to the street for attention, found it there—
tossed pink rubber balls at the electric wires,

bounced them to every song that rhymed.
We'd ransack garbage behind buildings, play
kick-the-can, play scummy with bottle caps.

Sidewalk was mother. *Asphalt*, father. Our parents
worked all day. We had chalk, Jan
could draw a real covered wagon. We all

jumped in, ate *Frank's Stand Hot Dogs* there.
Marsha drew a schoolroom! White oval
desk chairs in the street. When shadows reached

the spigots in the alleys we'd unscrew them,
let icy water come with a deep pipe sound.
We washed our bloody knees, and our grime.

The boy next door began to run his lanky,
schizophrenic circles, flapping arms
his neck, taut—*Unnhh* –he'd groan, and *unnhh*,

again—that cry, another pure fact of our world.
After dinner I sat on the front stoop picking
at the crunchy scab on my knee, the sky, a seaside

circus already wired for light.
More kids came, and someone's father
to burn our three-cent punks so we could

rid the neighborhood of mosquitoes, spend
the dark touching our match-struck sticks to wings.
Torching them down, all of us baring our teeth to fire.

—for Janice

Chloe Price Dance Studio

After tap class, I open the costume
closet to touch the row of tutus when
I spot a box, wrapped in cellophane
with a satin ribbon, the very same blue

as my eyes. It's stationery! Of course,
I have to have it, steal it outright,

fold it quickly into my reindeer sweater—
hide it in my dance
bag with my sweaty underwear, *8 and
1, 2 and flap step*—already inventing

the lie for my parents, *flap step*—
practice that lie the whole ten

blocks home—how a talent
scout had stopped me on
the street, *Little girl!* he was
calling, *Little girl!* from his

white top-rolled-up convertible—
*I want you to have this expensive
paper for your poems!* I practice
every word as I run, wonder

if I should mention the polka-dot
envelopes as I take up by twos

the tenement stairs, skip through
the front door whistling
Fats Waller, a detail no one
noticed, hustle that box

into my room, worry there beside
me on my bed! And why?

Because I plan to be Miss America
in the future, and after that,
a Rockette! O glory! O
sequin-dazzle top hat,

black high-heeled Chloe Price shoes
parting the breathless air—

when, at once, *shuffle-off-to-Buffalo*
ambition overtakes me—and my soul
speaks up—*Barbara Joan, you have
to take that stationery back!*

Puppeteering

The kids sit crowded on my bed
and I stand behind my desk which
I have pulled out from against my
wall, crouching as I am a little,
trying hard to work the marionettes
Uncle Bunny brought home for me
from Cuba, and I pull one string
and speak the boy's lines, moving
my lips and everything, speaking
for him dumb things like, "Hello
little girls" and "Buenas dias!"
and because I can't work
the two at once I have to lay myself
across my desk so I can look down
and see if he's moving, and all
the kids see I am no puppeteer,
despite my Uncle Bunny's confidence
in me and they grow bored too soon,
just when I'm figuring how I can
make her hand lift and lift, her hand
to his face, when my Mother comes in
as if nothing were happening and leaves
on my desk beside me, for my efforts
a big blue bowl of M&M's.

The Christmas Show

And just when I think the show is over, we must
kneel again and sing again—*We three
Kings of Orient Are*—I didn't want to
be a King in the first place. Plus all

three of the three wise men are Jewish girls.
Why is that? I love caroling through
the hallways soloing at every classroom
with the choir. Love decorating the tree

with things we'd drawn, but when I traced
the Trojan horse from the Library's *Book of Myths,*
teacher said I didn't really draw,
wouldn't hang it up at all. Christmas

is strange like that: When Miss Bibby got married
we had to call her Mrs. Flipping after
that. That is why she didn't give me the lead
in *Hansel and Gretel.* I lost that lead to Lois,

my mother's favorite friend of mine.
Lois' socks never slipped down into
her shoes like mine, slipped on account of my
skinny ankles, I guess. I had to be

not Gretel, though surely I was the best
singer in the whole fourth grade. Mrs. Flipping
made me be the Wicked Stepmother,
the only honest alto in the show.

Report Card

Barbara is not a good citizen,
Miss Bloom wrote. Aren't I the one
who helps the others in cursive writing?
Don't I always stand as proud as a flagpole
on the auditorium stage on Veteran's Day?
Isn't that American enough?
I am First Lieutenant of Safety Patrol,
first girl ever to hold the post, busiest
corner—Massachusetts Avenue
and Pacific, spreading my arms out
like gulls' wings. I glue my eyes to the light:
red, yellow, me standing the tallest
by green. Snap and I turned sideways,
waving my starched, gold-button-gloved hand
for the other schoolchildren to cross. Sometimes
I have to count on Nick, the traffic cop,
to stop a City bus for me. The whole
world, waiting and I, the Law's white harness,
girl with the spit-shined badge!
When I say *Go*, everyone goes.

One Sunday

I left the pigeons on the boardwalk, skated
home, one hand in my shorts pocket with
the folded handkerchief, my skate key on
a shoe lace tied in a bow around my neck.

In the vineyard of this memory it's a summer
Sunday, and the neighbors are coming to hear
my mother play her Schubert, and my father,
sing *St Louie Woman,* accompanied by her,

and his ukulele from the War. Late afternoon,
everyone listening, sitting in the dining room
on our kitchen chairs, and borrowed folding
chairs some had carried from home.

All of them staying after for my mother's
famous coffee and hazelnut cake, and for
my parents' ballroom dancing after that, he
dipping her backwards, like in the movies,

the Victrola in the living room playing softly,
my mother's hair just-washed, and gleaming,
as breezy as it had ever been. My brother and I
in the front row, side by side on the couch,

both of us proud, perfectly grateful for this—
his tapping fingers on his knee, my thinking
about pigeons, wondering about how late is
the love of birds—*Happiness!* Nothing less.

Pick-Up Games

The Social Studies teacher told my mother
I was *too aggressive* for a girl. Sure

I loved to climb the ropes in gym.
Gym was my favorite subject. Running

the track above had charms, believe me.
Did she think I was a boy? The bra

I bought with my mother at Lerners
was strappy and white as the throat

of a gull. I wore it to shoot baskets
after school. I wore it to play wire-ball,

stoop-ball, scummy on the sidewalk, flick
my souped-up bottle caps with my thumb

onto the chalk-drawn board. There were
bloody lessons there. When my father

came home from work, my mother
sent him to see. It was after dinner.

He told me to lift up my polka dot
blouse, show him my bra. I did,

and saw on his face what breasts were.

Rented

My brother
saves enough
money from
his paper
route to rent
us bikes we
can ride, dawn
until nine.
My brother—
who taught me
to dive in-
to breakers,
let myself
go under
come up to
prove I was
brave, set our
pace: side by
side, pumping
hard our legs
down the board-
walk, sea-crash
on one side,
the streets where
we live, on
the other.
The Light House.
The taffy,
the mini
golf course with
a hot dog
stand. We ride
past Planters
Peanuts, where

a machine
dressed up as
a peanut
in a high
hat grinding
nothing with
his spoon in
the hugest
Pyrex bowl.
We ride all
the way to
our mother's
shop where she
sits smiling
in the door-
way. Walk by
her window,
so crammed with
movie star
pictures she
took: Elvis,
Pat Boone, framed
Johnny Ray.
Her camera
gigantic,
the tripod
obscured by
her long black
veil. Click. *Chin
up, Barbara.*
Time runs out.
Bye Mom. So
we have to
race against

hungry, past
Mammy's, how
I want to
click our kick-
stands down. No
money. No
pancakes. O
my one and
only best
brother, my
own—I'll do
whatever
you say. Where-
ever you
want, I'll go.

My Brother's Closet

I am sick with fear of the dark,
the need-to-pee-but-won't-get-up fear
of the dark, my white sheets cold with
fear of dark sound, the sudden sharp
turns in the hallway, the threshold
to my brother's empty room,
his closet open, clothes tossed on the bed,
the ones not good enough for college.
I walk into his nearly empty closet,
I wrap myself in his leather jacket,
pushed my hands through his cuffs,
helped myself to his absence.
I rummage his silky pockets,
half a stick of gum, a folded
letter, pink, rippling, maybe love,
like a Sonnet from the Portuguese.

I sit on the edge of his maple bed,
read under my breath *Darling, feed me*
your dick, your dripping wet cock.
Betrayed! Me, flushed in his jacket
wrapped in the arms of my brother gone off
to college, his leathery smell, my own dark
need, the senseless sexless pull of blood.

Health Class

Swimming sperm, not fish,
not nearly fish, a drawing
of a weird armada, Viking
ships coming and only
one egg, like the sun.

I had no idea
what I was seeing.
The Health Teacher held
her stick to the screen to show
us that our bodies are lines,

not this warm skin I lick
on the back of my hand, not
the fine blonde hairs that grow there.
She had us copy a body
of words: *Vulva, Vagina,*

Clitoris and *Sex.*
We fell silent. *Penis.*
The whole class did. Even
the steel school door held still—
if someone breathed we didn't

notice. We didn't dare.
Was that snow just coming
down from the sky in the
window? Fear ran in
a tiny circle like a dodge-

ball. My hand pulled higher,
from under my skirt, my tights.
I closed my eyes to see
what life really was—

I thought of the first wave
that ever took me under, riptide
I had wrestled with all my strength.
Part of me drowned, made two
children of me in one. We were

not prepared, could not
pretend, small and helpless—
for we were children, both
of us. Until second
period, we hadn't known.

I Should've Had My Nose Done

when I was sixteen instead of using character
to pull me through the waiting and the hoping
to be chosen when I knew the girls with tiny

noses had it made. The ones with perfect
turns-up-the-ends were happy to be necking
at the drive-in making fog enough to fill front

windows and their panties while I watched
the movie in the backseat with my boyfriend.
Every senior knew which nose should stay

and which should go and though I loved
the company of noble Cyrano it was a tough
act to follow for a kid with aspirations,

like the dances and the parties, where my nose
gave up prominence to a boy's fat kisses
on my tongue. I knew that changes could be

made. Late at night I ironed away the steamy
wrinkles on my cotton blouse after trysting
in the backseat of a boy's father's car.

I believed in miracles, plastic surgery, black eyes,
the bandages, and courage of the fancy girls
who didn't have to work after school, the ones

who looked at me with such despair. O, my own
Pinocchio, where are the Snow White noses now,
that I have grown and you have stayed the same?

Lifeguard

The ice cream man who trudged the beach,
box roughly strapped by leather across his chest,
dropped sweetness at our feet, let dry ice steam
into the sky. I'd always buy an orange
popsicle on account of not really knowing
ice cream. We didn't have a proper freezer
in our fridge. Time to swim to the pole
that used to be a dock of the Grand Hotel.

I floated for a while out there. Then, swam
back in, was talking when the lifeguard called
me over to his stand—*Hey Barbara, do
you make out? Of course,* I said, not thinking,
just wondering a little what *make out* meant.
Could she tell, my mother, if I let
the lifeguard kiss me? I want him to kiss me.
He said he'd bring a beach towel for a pillow.

I'd never shared a pillow with a boy.
The sand was warm, I was new and starving
for his tongue. I was 13. It was
the summer that my father died, my mother,
crazy nearly, and the beach-chair-people still
wouldn't talk to me. I didn't know the stars then,
didn't know the hung-on-the-sea moon.
Afraid I was to look out. Unready to know.

Before Sputnik

We'd made a map of the whole United States
out of a piece of wood the size of our kitchen
table. With *Cray-Pas* I drew in the Rockies,
the San Joachim Valley, from pictures I'd
studied in books, while Norman Gasbarro painted

all the fields green. We glued on fancy letters,
named every National Park. We also
wired electric circuits to the giant battery
my brother brought home from shop class,
so that, when it was time, we could light up

each one with its own switch and tiny bulb.
And when it was our turn, we told, alternately,
and utterly competently certain highlights
of those parks, to the auditorium of kids
waiting to present their own final mysteries:

Carlsbad Caverns! (bulb on)—and I explained
the petroglyphs in the caves of *Bandolier!* (bulb
switched off) Norman said, *Grand Canyon!* (bulb
on) I said, *Grand Teton!* He said, *Yosemite!* and
demonstrated, with light and water, the ways of geysers.

(Bulb off) *Zion!* (Bulb on) places none of us would
ever be. No one could imagine what, in time,
would come: Absolute drought! The prairies turned
to sand, gray and stippled; ringlets which once were
rivers, westwarding to the very end of land—

We didn't say *earth* then. Before Sputnik, we said
America, our world... *from sea to shining sea.*

Wartime

1. Maneuvers

Do roses remember the journey
upward, earth's eyelid opening,
forcing them through? I was
conceived in wartime, in a hospital
bed tented with muslin sheets.
It was spring in North Carolina.
I was content to happen there,
a rosette in the whorl that passes
between cells. By June my mother
recognized me quicken in her
belly—she climbed into the bathtub,
wire coat hanger twisted open
in her hand. She wanted to undo me
but I clung to the wall inside her,
tucked up, refusing to be let go.
From the sound of things I knew
I'd better not breathe.

2. Call to Arms

I didn't want to. Heat pressed
the alveoli of my lung sac. I
whorled in that wrestle and I
pounded. I fought with my will,
which rose out of me—*No!*
but the tightening tightened,
took me by the waist, threw me
down—suck of the dam
before bursting, suck of the sun
and the sweetly bruising moonrise,
I did not realize my separate body
there. I licked my fingers, taking
what I could, then filled her with no intention

of staying. In my headstrong
pummeling, I exhausted her. Deserted her,
the girl she regretted
spilling out, once, and for all.

3. Battle Hymn

After that my life was an indulgence
of ordinary riches—
a cardboard toy box, the painted
carousel at the Amusements,
my brother's collection of stones.
Sometimes we'd sing around
our mother's piano. My father
played his wartime ukulele,
my brother, the Cuban
maracas. I danced, grew
gregarious, street-smart,
a perfectly aggressive child.
Sundays we'd all drive to the airport,
watch planes take off. My father
prayed to the God outside
the sunroom windows. I believed
in the *Book of Knowledge,*
everything there was to know.

4. The Spoils

On the couch, where the backs of
his fingers brushed
my breast. On the hassock where
I may have dropped my homework.
On the naked hallway floor.
In the kitchen where he turned
the corner to the wooden

thresh-hold of my room. On the
linoleum patterned to
be an Oriental rug.
On the bridge chair where my doll
was crying. On the cushion
where my doll was keeping all
her buttons buttoned. On my
flowered taffeta spread,
my Teddy deciding not
to love me. On my pillow,
my father talking to me
in a voice sadder than I
had ever, until now, known.

5. Reveille

I was sleeping in blue
seersucker pajamas and that
sleep was a deep forgetting.
I woke to thunder at the door.
I shook—leaf-tremble. Blue
body of a leaf-vein,
the face of fear was
a human face, my mother
in her nightgown
screaming. Was it
anger, that deep,
organic surprise?
I pressed hunger to my lips
with my thumbnail. I
made myself small. *Call
Aunt Bea* my mother ordered:
4-6-9-7-1. Hellowhoisthis?
When Aunt Bea answered,
I cried out, *Mama. What*

should I tell her—girl torn
like a plum from the branch, barely
ready—*Tell her*
your father is dead!

6. Purple Heart

In the living
room there was
a rose my
mother kept under
water, a souvenir,
bivouacked in a crystal
ball. Her coffee table
rose. Waxed and stemless,
blossom refusing to bleed,
ruthless in its dark
unfolding.

The Darkroom Man

He spends his days in moonlight,
dipping paper into pans of acid in a room
behind the Shop. All day he waits
for faces to appear one dimensional. The face
of summer develops slowly. First, sea
leaks in. Then sand, that souvenir exposed

beside the flat horizon. A woman artfully exposed,
seeps up to him from his pan of moonlight.
Vacations flood his page—the sundark sea
dragging the painted tide. From her motel room
she's come to buy a postcard of herself, her face
effaced in his stop-bath. He doesn't see who waits

on the other side of the darkroom door, waits
posed in the wicker rolling chair, exposes
her flowered bathing suit, her face
edged lovely by fluorescence. Fake moonlight.
Tourists hang on clothespins wired across the room.
Diluting him: *Take off your clothes.* The sea

demanding: *I am the Sea*
pounding in you. His mind waits
like the Flying Horse, making room
for emptiness, the palomino,
afraid to dive. The mind unscrews the red light-
half developing a woman, half-a-face

disembodied in the lens glass, his whole face
reflecting the mirrored dark. No sea
sounding where he stands. No moonlight.
He opens the *White Cottage Photo* door. Madness waits
suspended, undressed. *Kunstwollen* exposed.
He strides out naked. All time. All room

for revelation. The raw eye of the camera makes room:
His skin shines like holiness. His face,
a master plan, the gulls exposed.
Real pigeons yawn above the tin sea,
a vacancy. Even the sandpipers wait.
Vortex, or pinprick? He can't decide. True moonlight

relieved of dark rooms. Art needs light,
the woman's lips, exposed. He waits—
her drowned face rising from the backdrop sea.

Queen of the Nobodies

I don't really know what
a girl is supposed to do
when her father suddenly

dies. So I decide to
wear my party dress to his
funeral, and the garnet birth-

stone ring he gave me. Then they
close the coffin lid, I not-
on-purpose cry out—*But*

how can he breathe? Aren't I
supposed to give the Central
Junior High graduation

speech—I, the Queen of Nobodies, who helps the kids on
my block win the school

elections. We are the hard
workers from the tenements
on the wrong side—*We, the men*

of tomorrow, must take the
future into our hands. When
I go back to school, Miss Abary

calls me to the front of the
class. *Children*, she says.
Look hard at Barbara—

what has happened to her
could happen to you if
you think too much of yourself!

Comic Books

I read comic books, and I was the hero of comic books
—Elvis Presley

I read comic books to learn how to
live my life: Huey, Dewey, and Louie
hooked an umbrella handle to the blue
absolute of the sky, the sky buoying

them sufficient, so they could swim. I loved
especially Little Lulu, officious, bossy,
able to hold her chin high, even though
she had no neck. Strange things were possible.

Every UGH!! and GRR-H!! over Bluto's head,
dispatched by a can of spinach in Popeye's fist.
Whoever was bad, stayed bad. Good was always
good, not like in books where the tragic was

sure to happen and a kind person could turn
mean in the next chapter. I was a nervous
child, whose true heroics came at bedtime:
roaches scuttling the floorboards inside my walls.

Nonetheless, I'd make myself fall asleep.
In the morning there'd be Mickey smiling
beside my pillow, implacably, inevitably.
And Jiminy Cricket, fooling himself into fear-

lessness by whistling. And motherless Dumbo,
still flying, and motherless Bambi filling the frame
of the forest. Even Superman
was motherless, however disguised. I

scrutinized their painted expressions, clouds
above them carrying their every word.
They said what they'd do, then did. They could be
whatever they'd say. Their attributes running

ahead of them, one square box at a time,
a world not so much of confidence
but regularity, the geometry
of their noses and ears. Their every locution

an exclamation! Bravado in every intent.
I loved the accumulation of comic books
piled on my one bookshelf, the shining covers,
the two-cents used democratic paper,

the pages that smelled so good, accessible,
and satisfying. I came to comic books
the way I came to every pleasure—hopeful,
expecting everyone to somehow show

up next issue, gullible or square-
jawed, setting out again, unchanged,
a world of meek adventures, and the motto:
First, you fail. Then you get redeemed.

Painted Horse on the Carousel

The ones who come to ride
kick my flanks, and saddle
me with hurtings, chase me
from here to kingdom-come.
I will not take the bridle.
Even if they press shut my snout.
Even if they pull my ears, pain
is the fury I thrive on. I am
hoof-kick, the chestnut force
of life hereafter, the once
and utter certainty. The hot,
raw center of the business.
My body stands where it is,
meets its assignments, life
by life. As I was made to.
As I want to.

II. TRANSPARENCY

Monarch in a Jar

1.

Light made seeing easy—
the sun falling under.

I could tell by two spots
that it was a male. All night

I had to calm him, to keep
his wings from tearing. I lay

in my bed beside him,
in his jar.

He hung quite still.
I could hear his breath

resting. His wings,
drying geometries.

By dawn I could see
pink tips, shades of stasis,

a double undoing.
Something new.

2.

Last Tuesday I watched the caterpillar
climb the smooth glass wall

of the jar, quickly
choose its spot

on the branch

I had stood in there,

and he hung
onto it attached

by the very top of his head,
tail curled up into

a capital letter, *J*. All
of it clinging by gossamer,

matter of another kind.
No more to be striped hunger.

3.
What happened next
was the shaking. It trembled

horribly, convulsing
the curvy swoon, shocks

of celadon winding,
until it was not

itself anymore, but jade.
It shined, that stone. It pouted

wetly. And seemed hard, though
I didn't touch it.

Chrysalis, the first
puzzle piece,

a signal flag bound
to the self

it couldn't know.
And within itself, an assistant-

self, throat ringed
with beads of gold.

I feared it would fall off
the branch, so heavy it seemed.

Still, it held, shook there a while
in the work of its living.

4.
I stayed up all night
with it as it turned blue.

Darker blue. Darker, into
the sheer air of transparency.

Hints of shape pressed
and folded like a lavendered

bed sheet. Something
in there was moving

the way something moves,
or not, in every political direction.

Then I heard
a blue kind of softening.

Years of nights I used
to breathe beside

the faces
of my children. I was

nothing but lullaby then.
I stared and I stared, when

suddenly, I could see inside
a host of miniature, Origami

stained-glass wings I almost
took for the face of God!

5.
Noon, precisely. I carried the jar outside,
across the street to a neighbor's

garden, those asters billowing.
I took off the screen I'd devised

roughly as a lid, to set him
flying, but he didn't go.

I coaxed him with my voice.
He climbed out over the lip

of the jar (I couldn't believe this!)
out onto the back of my hand,

and farther, onto my wrist,
onto my forearm where he stopped,

every weightless speck of him
working the map of his celestial

mind, routing himself,
ingeniously, due south.

6.

I didn't really see him go,
maybe a spark in the trees

behind my house. Green fact,
blue, jubilant world,

let me too be flung out, wholly
new, into that selfsame lucky span.

III. PROOF OF THE SPINNING WORLD

Cro-Magnon: Day One

The new brain brought
with it a new
idea: *bury*
your dead, which stopped
our trek. So we
could dig the holes
into which we
could toss our kin—
perhaps with care.
Then grave markers
arrived. And, most
likely, love, which
was not much more
than notice of
another to
kneel beside, to
want to see it
breathe. Then not breathe.
It would be ten
thousand more years
until Grief—

Steeplechase

Lower the shovel and flatten the ground.
                              —Gerald Stern

Mostly, denial, my nerves
in abeyance—add
one day and a stoop sets in.
I churn my shoulders to undo it,
but stooping stays.

It has happened. The present
edits the past, and I am loosed
from my brother like when we rode the whip
at Steeplechase Pier, sitting tightly
together in the steel blue car, our hands

glued to the safety bar, he, so big
his knees came nearly to his chin.
And I, loudly laughing, and weren't we
safely going slowly, begun slowly,
until the fact kicked in.

Murder the stones, smooth,
or rough grey, or otherwise. Kick hard.
Kick the dirt and make it spin.
My brother doesn't care a fig,
though dirt is washing his tears.

Dirt, filling his mouth, opened
slightly, despite the stitches
of mortician's thread—
The shovel is done.
The man in the box is a goner.

The Work of Shoes

Shoes touch earth on our behalf.
Shoes hold us smooth on tarmac
or on stones. Shoes comfort us
in puddles, and help us cross.

New shoes win us from outside
shoe store windows—in we go
to try them on—by looks alone
we love them. Or else we don't.

Expensive sheepskin shoes.
Pointy toe cowboy shoes, used,
shoes with unsayably high heels.
Gym shoes and work shoes, new

shoes that win us by looks alone.
Shoes touch the earth on our behalf.
Dress shoes, worn, graveled on
sidewalk stones, smooth shoes for

dancing, red shoes, shoes blue,
or Plath black. No shoes allowed
to grieve a Jew. No Jew allowed
to be buried in shoes—too far to run.

Things in Their Disorder

Toss a stone
and you will never be able to

stop that fire. You may have
meant nothing by it.

You wanted only the toss.
Not the tension. Not the twinge,

unrealized, unnecessary. That release,
that error in judgment is God.

B'reshith, Revised

Chapter 1

The need for tables had not arisen. We took our meals on the grass.
We stood our vases on the grass and left our books out, open. We
had no knick-knacks yet, as travel had not been invented. We stayed
close to the hut circle, and to the caves. We obeyed the light—faced
it as we worked, we slept when it turned away. The push to bed had
been satisfied with straw. For a tooth brush we used our fingers. Time
went on. One day the sun tables arrived. It took a week to unwrap
them, all marble and Venetian glass, and from the northern region,
teak and rosewood. So many tables, we built for them a house. This
we called *Tabernacle.*

Chapter 2

Then came water: the Red Sea filling up with it, the other seas
already full. Our bodies likewise. And certain bath tubs, punch
bowls, and trash cans after storms. They too full, and water behaved,
grumbling and stirring, unable to climb. *Sink. Sink,* it told itself.
Split. Tear, it cried. Down is its measure and down is its song. Even
an ark floated above its own stinking hold. A whale rose and set
herself, and rose again.

Chapter 3

We went in as if nothing unusual had happened. All of a sudden,
the need to orient the self to circumstance. Where to stand? Where
to gather shells from the tide? We lived as we lived, uncyclical in
our revisions, writing by candlelight. But how to think in the cellar
of beingness, when it's damp down here, and we've finished the
wine? And weren't we sad for a few missing things: movie theaters,
cigarettes, guns?

Chapter 4

Rabbi Akiba went out into the desert looking for the resolution of history. Looking, too, to resolve the problem of his aching teeth: *Think of us,* they said. His throat was parched: heart-line, brain-pulse—and, besides books, what would become of his sorry predicament? His wife wanted servants, his son, an ample inheritance. Besides a good name, what had Akiba done with his one and holy life?

Chapter 5

We receive only our due. What kind of God comes up with such a deal? Everyone lives a myth, heroes with their snake piles, each Siren on her own lustrous island. Though the rest of us are petulant in our indulgence we do not abandon the air we are recirculating. God has a penchant for the cyclical, so is slow to anger. How to live on the surface and not turn the story into ours alone? God, an imperious sort pulls back on the reins of any wagon, such petulance, cynical. Do we slip away then, godly, recording ourselves, as we see in this revision?

Concerning Slugs

Two slugs have mistakenly dragged
themselves to my doorstep. I find them

writhing naked there, scoop them up
in my backyard shovel carry them across

the road to the field, trees bending
to the keel of the sun. Pears swollen,

resistant, self-deluded, past satisfying
on the branch. I want to save the slugs.

Deliver them to their new damp hiding.
Slide them off the shovel to the ground—

they do not move. Have I hurt
them? Have I torn them from their

just-hatched young left sleeping
under the lattice-shadowed porch?

Who will teach them what to feed on now?
Earth has a penchant for the not-just-yet,

spinning the very start of things, giving
up to certain orphans—slugs

for instance, what they need. As it did
for me in my shameless, dark unfolding.

Poem at Split Rock Cove

Brushfire—watching
fire as if it were
sunrise yellowing—
Say what you see, says
the fire. I study
the beach, rockweed
tangled in stones. Pull

at the barnacles
attached to the stones.
I squeeze bulbous seeds
that refuse to yield.
Resist, the rockweed
cries from the daily
apocalypse. *Hold*

to things slow, and hard,
says the tide. *Believe*
in the hard, says the
hard. The people in
chairs sit on. A whale
blows in the harbor,
lifts its life without

us in mind. Nothing
is as it seems—not
the five who stare at
fire, not tide loudly
lapping the fishing
pier, not the ladders,
not even the pile

of empty lobster
traps, not expecting

a thing at all, though
the paint-peeled buoy
is bobbing. *Be fair,*
says the buoy. *Look
again,* says the sky.

Before the Meteors

1.
Taos, high on the mountain, steady
wind, the gorge torn already through.
Below the bridge, moose roam. Or
are those big-horn sheep? In any case,
how did they get down there?
I recognize nothing is stable today.
High on the bridge I stand noting
the upright piano someone threw over
the iron railing—unremembered for years,
but not tomorrow, though surely
there was a tomorrow then.
I must live without expectation,
work as hard as raindrops work
no reason to be prepared.

2.
There are lichen here
that join at the hip
and not lichen only.
That one is algae
and they consort as one
taking the stones
taking the guard rails and the gate
they keep their DNA to themselves
neither pleased enough with the other
to give their pith away—
asexual some call it. Though it sounds
like sex to me.

3.
No idea of how far I have walked,
how far I have to walk in return,
to be this free: No boundaries, no street

signs, no road. Passing the world and letting
it go. Green it is. And red. And the one
school bus, as yellow as ever. The sky is too
high, the sea too low. I walk between
the layers, consigned to my own two feet.
My whole body propelled by the zillion
muscles that make me stand.

4.
I always choose the storm.
Would choose it again.
To be out in it. To be certain
of nothing but the storm
iceberg ice that blue. Only pelting
and pelting and it isn't personal,
has nothing to do with me.
Most things we choose we don't
know we are choosing. I choose
the storm as a wolf might choose the
highroad or low road for the sake of pack.
He thinks low and all of them go.

5.
In less remote places I have found myself.
But my best hope was Antarctica. That ice,
the three suns,
those three suns, and the green sky.
Beneath the ice
an entire continent, houses and forests
and all of the children practicing magic.
The cataclysm let some of us go.

6.

Before the meteors, some of us climbed trees.
Some of us floated out on ice floes
to South America. Picked up the language quickly.
Some of us were friendly, others, political
in the sense of being more or less congenial,
personal, walking in anyone else's shoes. To
balance on their uneven floors. The few
and far between throw rugs. To enter
the life of another is to love.

7.

At the antipodes of the mind we are
more or less completely free
of language, wanting nothing of words
at all. Gestures live as they did
in prehistoric time. Kiss, touch, murder,
make a fire and the antipodes will tremble.
Play opera on the turntable. Maria Callas
singing *Norma,* the antipodes feel strangely
talkative. We expect our children to speak,
hope they will have a thing or two to say.
Then surely we forget to listen or, if we've read
Freud, think we listen but
don't, though I'd meant to.

8.

We are curious by nature. Human beings
need to strive, even if we are hip,
and glib; Even if we never let on we are
innocent, which is not, is happy in
and of itself. We reject happy. That, too,
is our nature. We need to exercise our wits.

East Boston Federal Courthouse

I stare at the face of my son
his eyes wildly innocent as he
drags by—in-chains—ankle to ankle,
wrist to wrist, his shoulders pulled
so far up his back there must be bruises

bearing down. Because his lawyer said
such things could move a judge to leniency,
I took in a homeless cat who, from the start,
lacked the genetic gift of movement.
We called her *Amerika.*

She'd fly across the room to bite me,
fly across the room while
I was reading—to bite my wrist, a kind
of play, I thought, only too aggressive.
But I misjudged her. I'd never heard her purr,

never imagined, sitting so close behind
the trouble of my son. Now and then
the cat would let me touch the top
of her head. But mostly she'd walk away.
Or cry out, or call me maddeningly

from the bowl. To make her happy I'd open
the front door, or plug pheromones
like a nightlight into the wall.
I began to wonder if she'd do well
on a farm somewhere, began to take

the feral fact of her to heart. Helpless
in the Federal Courthouse in my row.
I suffer with my son who must
somehow answer the curt D.A.—
and didn't you tell the detective then....

My breath is a wail inside my chest,
wall to wall. What was it made me keep
the cat who bit me bloody? The vet advised
me to surrender her to a shelter.
This animal cannot live with people, she said.

Hard to Tell

-for my grandson, Jed

You are lost to me, precious one,
black-eyed truth I used to sing to.
Here's a story you don't know. A son
fell into the sea, or seemed to.
But it was really we, rolling backwards. Not meaning to, not wanting to,
your father swept into maelstrom, the wrack
of waves. Cold injustice, the courts, too,
gone awry, the winds tied up in weeds,
the shambles of high tide. You too, swept up.
Dusk clings to what is. Grandeur believes
in convergence. We are not close enough.
I hope you'll know substantiated sun
not wearing that sky-blue-pink illusion.

Moth in Three Voices

1. Stephanie

I held through
dusk to her
window screen,

just a moth
watching (street-

light show me
up.) She turned
off her lamp

to see me, so
I sang *Somewhere
Over the Rainbow.* Her
face was rain. *Baba,*

she spoke. *You have
the most beautiful voice
in the world.*

When she woke
it was dawn.
I was gone.

2. Emily

*Baba, is
that you?* she
cried out in

dream. And I
came and turned

on her lamp.
She was half
awake. I sighed

Go to
sleep my sweet,

lullaby-
my lovely curly girl,
my night-light child.

3. *Kayla*

Her light
turned off,
sky ripened

into dark.
My wings splayed

against her
window. *Is*
that you, Baba? I

held itself
still by my

feet. Feathered
eyes on each

unseeing wing. I was

her flickering
student, come
to her to learn

what there is
to believe.

To Be Happy

Can we always believe our own
eyes? And why not? And mustn't
we, for who are we if we do not?
Obey yourself is the final lesson,
though many of my teachers thought
otherwise. *Barbara, be quiet! Barbara
sit still! Barbara do not tend to your
neighbor. Janice will find a pencil
for herself!* Obey yourself, I'm
thinking now that I'm grown
and life has had its way with me.
Know thyself, a Greek said. *Heal
thyself,* another. Go on and be
bossy! Tell yourself what to do,
and do it. It's the first intention
that's the hardest. Make life up
then force your eyes to see it.
Look up, then bend to your task,
hard. Harder. Hardest happy.

Blood. Breath. Whisky.

Monument du Corps-Franc, Fontbruno, France

Someone saw the forest falling. And is gone—

Tonight, over Muscat
in dusty glasses, Julien salutes
his French Resistance—

boys toppling a hay wagon sullied
with soldiers and guns, stopping
for a while the makeshift war—

grape vines, honey-plaited bees, so loud
the river, so deep the stones. Same
old story. How sunflowers sometimes

stand up to rain. Even lunatic dragonflies
shudder the crypt—everyone's name
stamped on the wall.

One must meet oneself regardless.
Let a dog come if he wants to.
We are all without permission.

The Trouble with Wealth

The way it divides space
into two teepees and at the top,
and bottom, two skies, like in
a house without windows but
within a courtyard and a total
rural sun. Two pools in every
Chinese house and in each
pool swim koi, because the word
koi is the same as the word for
wealth and since both are
pronounced the same way, no
one knows if koi is said in
the name of luck and happiness,
or in the name of acquisitiveness,
money buying the many elaborate
Chinese bed frames, and the rice
pans, the portable heat braziers,
the tall ceramic pickle jars, and
after Mao, the guns.

The Generals

Let them blow Korea off the map. That oily hole
might have heft. Could be Afghanistan. Let them return
three places in the Czech Republic. And no one who lives
there can find the bus. Divide Russia, or let it implode.
Change the names of everything to Uzbekistan—
suddenly the cobbler shuts his door and the grocer
has no beets. Not even an artichoke. Even the stamps
at the post office are spouting volcanos. Whatever
lava knows is also true. *My country* depends on
the speaker. It could be Syria. It could be Mexico.
The children in refugee camps bless each other
as if they were God. Step out into the quiet night.
Leave the door open behind you.

Boston Marathon Bombing, 2013

A sunny day in Back Bay, the runners, proud,
crowds watching the jurisprudence of limbs
fly off. Once it was oil-boiling cauldrons
dumped from battlements and swords, stones for stoning.
Trees: swamp oak, white oak, hickory, native

woods made into bows and arrows, black
walnuts carved into guns. The race has become
an arsenal of pressure-cooker bombs
for lacing flesh with flares. And nails. And chips
of glass. And carpenter's tacks. Bombs

made by hand, instructions on the in-
ternet by brothers who won scholarships
to college, played basketball together after,
carried groceries for neighbors at home.
Troops came in a swath as wide as a city bus.

Humvees. The Metropolitan Police.
Orpheus moved boulders by the power
of his lyre. People wept with that beauty.
They believed Eurydice would follow,
though love lives as the dead live, milling

about Commonwealth Avenue. The trees
in bud, the traffic sleeping, the sidewalks full
of blood. Knapsacks indistinguishable
in the everywhere surveillance. The State
ready to pounce, to wrap itself in the flag.

Falling

I stand by the gurney where my son lies
dying. The curtain is weeping.
I watch his life proceed. *Brian!*
It's Mom. And he tosses the branch
of his arm upon me. I kiss the bloody
blossom of his hand. *Hineni*, I say

to the parched earth of his mouth
sweating from every tooth-root, his
broken, ruined jaw; both shoulders
twisted above the sheet. I kiss the fever
between his brows. I kiss his hair. I kiss
his silk-backed ear. His breath is

trampled unconscious. They say
he fell from a third story balcony.
I conjure the balcony in Córdoba, wooden
synagogue of Maimonides, where women
climb to pray, everything smelling
of garlic. Of olives. Of rotting heat.

It was an angel met Brian at birth, hard snap
of fingers above his upper lip, that human
crevice, to mark the one come shouting out
into the brittle world. I consoled him by touch
even then. Falling is another matter. Light waits
like a boulder to be up this mountain pushed.

Boston, Midwinter

Even if fear makes the kiss
tremble. Even if scent spits

its relentless *I am,* love
may turn you to stone, or glass

if you're not careful. Even
glass seeks its other.

Stars are unafflicted. All day
they gaze toward nostalgia.

Winter's sun is a poor ghost
of itself. The sky is cold all

the time. How then
to be happy? Come to love

open armed, slowly
so as not to be burned.

Even alleyways happen to
gleam, though fire escapes

slant so brightly we must look away,
into drifts. Snow accumulates

on the windows. Bent to its task.
Hard. Harder. Even snow.

The Cat, Beauty

She swats at her little snowman—his mouth is gone,
and most, but not all of the catnip inside: perfume
of primal attachment. It takes little for her to be
happy—

the front door opening, the threshold
shining—lick of a paw, other paws
saved for the carpet's luxury.

Nights she ambles to make sense of the day.
When I bathe, she comes to test the edge.
And why not? If I sigh before sleep, she jumps up
to the pillow beside me,

breathes me, lets her tail
touch my animal hair. Outside, the cold proceeding,
night longing, the leaves falling and the leaves
partaking, each one with its own true sound.

Last Evening

Attention must be paid.
                                    —Arthur Miller

It didn't merit celebration, just
that I decided to sleep in
the bed again, and rose
in darkness from the reading
chair, performed some
ablutions, then pulled
back the covers and sat
down on the sheets.
I lifted my legs, slid
under covers, turned
off the bed light, lay
for a while, the pillow
surprising my hair.
Face the ceiling without
thought or merit. Trucks
come and go in the street.
I smile a little. Or I don't.
I sense the armoire of my body,
seek the key. Have rest come
like unwilling children, called
home before dark.
Faced right. Faced left,
and soon it was tomorrow.
I swear I wanted to
celebrate my return
to the customary, but
was unaccustomed
to self-congratulation,
so rose quickly into
the new day. In this
note to myself,

without forethought
or erasure, I declare
that I have changed.

Walking Without an Umbrella in New York City

Don't worry, I say to the fallen man
bleeding onto the subway's stairs.
You're OK, I say from the gutter
of my throat. I kneel beside him.

We wait together for sirens in the rain.
What's in the way, rain accommodates,
grazes the grey of the man's mustache,
lends the city's sidewalk *panache.*

Ceaseless rain runs. *Don't worry,* I say
to the bride, sobbing soaked under
the Plaza's soaking awning, the train
of her gown lapping sludge, her groom

beside her, holding his wind-blown
umbrella. He is broken. She is angry.
Don't worry, I say to their worry.
The first twenty-five years are the hardest!

Floods

The morning had begun with rain.
I found my boots in the hall
closet, slid one on—shook out
from the other what seemed to be
a leaf—but what fell was
my son's pet newt, stiffened,
dead in there. I hadn't noticed
the lightning, leaf-tips paling,
the sound of groans.

I was born in a caul. My father had
a rabbi come to bless me. When I was
nine, he hired someone to test my
clairvoyance. She sat at the kitchen
table beside me, shuffling cards.
I was shy with her. She told me
to predict the king of hearts—
  You will never drown.

The day my husband left forever,
the ceiling in his office caved
under the press of the upstairs shower,
horsehair plaster shredding his
upholstery—he was lugging trash
bags of his sweaters to the front door.
I cried out to him *It's raining
in your office.* He shouted back—

  Your flood!

The Cliffs

—Trinity Bay, Newfoundland

Because my friend said *Let me show you,* we drove
    for miles of unpaved road until the shale
        and rocks stopped us. Roughly. The sea was grey

      and spackled. Summer buttoned my sweater red.
    We had come to the green end of the world. Earth
was the equation and there were flowers, wild-

      crazy blossoms spun from a single stalk.
    We lay on the juniper to watch for whales—
        I lay here naked once, she whispered,

beside my shy husband. I grew still in respect
    for her sorrow until a foghorn flooded
        the oceanic roar. Horizon was

      an imagined island rising. Ice battered
    the coast's invisible tide. Nothing beyond.
        Only out—   out and far were all.

Girl on a Wheel

Was it love, the desperation I was
feeling, terrible, and tearless?
I unzipped the oxygen tent,
leaned inside to kiss my cousin's eyes,

her lids burning-up, burning raw,
no one there to help me with that fire.
Waiting is a wheel. I move to the center
to feel less the spin. I was sixteen, before

I'd read Kierkegaard and the Jewish mystics,
though even they draw a blank at the nub.
From nothing into nothing. One cough.
Her lungs gave out without a word.

A person lives. Then she doesn't.
This isn't modern. Her mother used to
let us play cash register with the ice
cube trays and real nickels and dimes.

Ilean, it's the most perfect spring.
There is no destiny until one turns,
looks back, every breath an echo
just as soon forgotten.

My father always said I had her
kindness. But was there anything not
in me from the beginning?
Anything reserved for later?

i.m. Ilean Fran Goldstein
1944-1961

After Reading Da Vinci's Notebooks

I scan my face in the bathroom mirror,
begin with the sockets of my teeth.
Trace a line from my ear
to the bony arch on the side of my skull—
this is the human franchise, how the jaw

gives in to age. The body has its reasons.
Susceptible as it is, my heart to wild
derangements, is insensible to touch.
My lungs seem to proceed from outside force.
There is no arbitrary here.

If I crouch down to pick up a penny
near the curb, won't impression register
itself unformed, a surge of leaves
becoming visible in the agitation
of my remotest muscle,

or in the hoopla of my nerves?
Maybe I've grown accustomed
to myself. Isn't every life
a work of resistance, battering
the great gears of the body down?

The Cat, Truth

For her excellence depends on no apparent
dignity, rather the genetic gifts of movement,
lithe as the tideless lakes of Africa, a face
that shows no feeling. Such is the cat
who may make her way as mayor or king,
shaking hands with riff-raff, or walking
by aloof as a summer lifeguard up
in his lifeguard stand. Excellence lay
in the will of the creature who does
as she wants, sleeps when and where,
plays with a torn leaf when she wants.
And yet I think she loves, and when
she purrs it is proof, and when she leaves
my side because I touch her for my own
sake, it is proof as well.

Light Takes the Tree

We stood, my child and I, waiting
for the late bus to come, when he ran,
impulsive, out into the street to meet it.
I had to run hard to catch him, and
the queue, swollen with strangers
dispersed to run out with me, into
traffic, the man in the yellow slicker
sweeping him up, my boy a football
under his arm. Then everyone laughing
applauding relief, ambling into line,
patting softly one another's shoulders,
and Eric, too, laughing among the leaves
as sodden as his own golden hair.

I watched from the far side of the bus, light
take the trees, the leaves leaving, one gold
Spartan at a time, each leaf a shark, like
in the school of sharks we see beneath
the bridge, six sharks circling the icy
Wiscasset, airing the spikes on their backs.
They were dark. They seemed to be solving
the problems of the world, or
was it hunger, their teeth so well prepared?
I knew by the way they bore their silence
they were sharks. Everyone else on that bus
said they were porpoises. They were not.
The ocean is so rich with white-fleshed
fish, easy to spot a stock of sharks in rain.

A man obeys the instinct he was born to,
whistles at a woman who's just stepped
into the bus, shaking rain from her hair.
At first he watches her breasts, then her hips,
belly, calculating the likelihood of her

ability to bear his child, so young,
so lovely. *Get away from him.*
I'm thinking. She pulls the cord to stop.
Always that whiff of brimstone.
Sharks have no other option.

Dinner Conversations

—after Marianne Moore

Chicken soup and rice
for dinner that night. Full and steaming bowls sufficed
the appetite for food and consolation as
we joined around the table,
all together, all alone.

The conversation
rambled, then stopped at the firstborn's observation:
I don't want to be in a family anymore.
It's too complicated. We
stared down into the parsley

in our bowls, red trays
carried from the kitchen, the silver set for one.
Candles stayed lit bravely. The baby cried for more.
His father passed the honest
bread, scraped the plates when we were

done.

Fortune Teller

I can tell you only what you know.
You may be right.

Set your own crystal upon the table,
I have.

Then read the signs.
There is a road. And I am looking down.

For what?
For stars.

Will they be found?
I think I'm owed.

How long have you been looking?
Very long.

Still, you hope?
Still I hope.

Won't you give up then?
I have given up.

You do not seem to understand
This is my predicament.

The value of despair.
O, predicament!

Do you mean contingency?
Yes, also that.

Latitude 40 North

No road signs, no instructions
in the glove compartment, no
way to shift into reverse

the rented Renault. The moon
is full and screaming *Orange*
over onion fields. The sky—

not black exactly—mottled
like a dog. There seem to be
ditches ahead on both sides.

I could read, by the visor's
tidy lamp, unreadable
maps. I could try singing, or

eat dried apples from the bag,
but real Danger's too thin to
swing around—*think dancing, think*

dandelions come up through
a sidewalk crack, despite the odds.
Isn't it possible for

things to come out right? Maybe
someone's set out to find me!
Are those lights in the distance

as steady as stars? *Think stars*
before there was cosmos. Who
has not been lost in this world?

—*for Wendy Drexler*

To Be a Sloth

Life is a lesson in humility
                    —James Barry

So sweet up there, moving rarely,
waking rarely, and I climbed up, dared up
balanced even without a tail,

bound by gravity swaying me   slowly
on one dumb dare. My whole self
                              out on a limb.

Unrhythmed. Unrhymed. Clumsy even.
Who will love me now that I
have shown how brave I am?

Night Guided by a Brown Beetle

She has waited through dusk to call herself
to my attention, porcelain back shining *See
me.* So I stop to watch her be. I could lie
on cobblestones beside her. I could
touch the inner membrane of her eye—

Revelation! Perceivable Premonition!
The Holy Painted Unity
made red by the soil of wine.

She is as real as the moon, floating
among dead leaves in the children's pool,
over-confident like a glowworm.
Or is she full of yearning
as she darkens, more like me?

Girl, Port Au Prince

These are the fine deeds of tenderness...
—René Depestre

One day the earth will not be,
and the fish who are waiting

to forgive the sea will drown,
the whole coast torn away. And

in the heart of trees a song will rise
to which even God may listen—

is that a nightingale?—
No one sees her standing

like a tinsel star.
A girl sweeping out the caterwaul

of dust. Ash swoops across
the blackening sky.

If she weeps at the brief dusk
and thinks of her family

is it our fault or is it what keeps
her steady in the dark?

Dust is her legacy, the urns
spilled out. All-things

live on the knife's edge.
Ask any soldier—

the battle will lose itself.
Night will never loosen its pearls.

The River Dure

I have come to suffer
the bark-streaked world
where toads call out
in the riverdark, all that
effort to find one another
waiting wetly on river stones.

The *Dure* renews itself by that
sound, time taking itself so
seriously. I will stay and be
made of staying. Let the river.
Let the cold. There is too much
world to fail. I will sleep

the night, glad to be sleeping, glad
to wake myself, like always, like
never before. No whispers. No breath
on my neck. Let love wait
like an umbrella in its stand—there
may be no rain. There may be no need.

Proof of the Spinning World

on the Provincetown Ferry

What I want is lightning as we whip
the turn from good to wild.

And seabirds, every one shining,
low-flying the trammel of clams,

the whole blue-black swath
as one, at once, breaking the dusk

like a bell, crying out their strange
elation among the mackerel clouds,

the air a monolith, a creed—
I stand watchful on the upmost

deck while the sky bruises—red
sun leaning into hard, audible

rain. Come thunder and thrill
sets in. The moon slips out,

silvered, sultry, that kind of
otherwise beauty, and in the face

of it, a certain callousness.

Acknowledgements

Gratitude to the following journals where these poems first appeared:

AGNI: "The Summer My Mother Said She was Going to Drown Herself"

Hudson Review: "Cro-Magnon: Day One", "Poem at Split Rock Cove" and "Latitude 40 North"

Ibbetson Street: "Highwire"

J Journal: "Blood. Breath. Whiskey."

The Lily Poetry Review: "The River Dure"

Muddy River Review: "Boston, Midwinter", "East Boston Federal Courthouse", "In the Dark", "Moth in Three Voices" and "Trinity Bay"

Prairie Schooner: "I Never Said I Love You Best" and "Night Guided by a Brown Beetle"

Radcliffe Quarterly: "Dinner Conversation"

Salamander: "Steeplechase" and "Wartime"

Sojourner: "Pick Up Game"

TAB: "Making Do"

Anthology:
Bared: Contemporary Poetry on Bras and Breasts. ed. Laura Madeline Wiseman. Les Femmes Folles Books; WV, 2016

9 781957 755045